Walking connects you to the countryside as no other means of transport can. When I moved to Bishops Stortford a few years ago, I knew nothing about the area or the subtle beauty of its landscapes. More than a thousand miles later, I have explored almost all the local paths, in every season, and this little booklet is, in part, a celebration of those ongoing adventures.

It is also a guide to a long, circular walk, the southern section of the Harcamlow Way, a 140-mile figure-of-eight walk, devised in the late 1970s by Fred Matthews and Harry Bitten. The whole route, as the name hints, runs from Harlow to Cambridge and back and is marked on Ordnance Survey maps. You need leisure maps 194, 195 and 183. Although there are no dedicated Harcamlow waymarks, these are all public paths with signs or arrows of some sort.

In one or two places (especially in the last section), I have deviated slightly from the original route, mainly to avoid spending too long near main roads. This 63-mile southern loop covers the section between Harlow and Newport. The Newport–Cambridge instalment will be published in 2015.

There is so much to enjoy along this route: the view from a rolling, Hertfordshire hilltop across a little river valley; or walking through the colourful houses that line the main street in medieval Thaxted; the craft workshops at Parndon Mill or the flowery expanses of Hatfield Forest; bluebells in Quendon or snowdrops at Easton; thatched cottages and Georgian mansions; the remains of an abbey at Tilty with a beautiful carved window in the old gate chapel, or the ruined tower at Thundridge near the village of Cold Christmas …

Leaving the car behind will make the walk feel more exciting and helps protect the environment you're enjoying. Bus routes and pubs will change, but I have listed the current ones as starting points. The website http://www. travelinesoutheast.org.uk/ is invaluable for checking travel plans and it's worth calling ahead if you're relying on stopping somewhere for refreshments.

Every time of year is beautiful along the Harcamlow Way, although wet weather will mean muddy stretches. May is especially lovely as woods and hedgerows overflow with birdsong and blossom; the lanes are laced with cow parsley and the fields with golden buttercups. Here are some seasonal highlights and I hope you enjoy them as much as I did.

Phoebe Taplin, 2014

Snowdrops in Easton The gardens of Easton Lodge (p. 18, http://www.eastonlodge.co.uk/) have dedicated snowdrop days in February. You can take a lovely circular walk from The Stag in Little Easton, past the church and ponds, to Easton Lodge and back along country lanes, fringed with catkins. You can also find carpets of snowdrops in Quendon Woods and in Debden churchyard.

Spring gardens in Harlow March and April are a good time to explore towns and villages, full of daffodils and tulips, and avoiding too much mud. Harlow Museum's walled garden (http://www.science-alive.co.uk/harlow-museum/) is an unexpected delight and the Gibberd Garden, with its many sculptures, is open from Easter each year (http://www.thegibberdgarden.co.uk/). You can walk between the two, through Old Harlow, and circle back to Harlow Mill (p. 5).

Bluebells in Quendon Several woods and tree-lined paths along the route have patches of bluebells in April and May. One of the best places to catch them is near Quendon. A little circuit from the Cricketers Arms at Rickling Green makes a lovely bluebell walk. Stroll through the glorious woods to the east of the B183, then cross the road and visit the small church, returning via the Harcamlow Way as on p. 12.

Music and morris dancers Thaxted (p. 15) is a beautiful town at any time of year. The summer months bring the added bonus of Thaxted Festival (http://www.thaxtedfestival.org.uk/) and morris dancing weekends, and the 19th-century windmill is open from Easter to September (http://www.thaxted.co.uk/content/windmill). There are lots of walking possibilities; one short circular route is to walk downhill from the windmill and back along the River Chelmer.

Ghosts and gold leaves From the bright beeches in Manuden to the burnished oaks of Hatfield, this walk glows with autumn colour. The hills near Thundridge (p. 7) are great for autumnal views and the spooky ruined church is riddled with Halloween tales (http://totallyhaunted.co.uk/cold-christmas-church.php). You can start from the Sow and Pigs pub in Thundridge (http://thesowandpigs.com/), walk to Barwick Ford and return via country lanes and golden beech woods.

Frost in the forest A circuit through the ancient hunting grounds of Hatfield Forest (p. 19) and along the frozen lake is a bracing winter walk. The cosy Green Man in Takeley (http://thegreenmantakeley.com/), with its coffee shop and cakes, makes a good starting point. Follow the broad woodland tracks and tarmac lanes to the outdoor café, which also serves hot drinks.

Sawbridgeworth to Roydon

7 miles

Apart from the historic, flowery meadows of Pishiobury Park, this first section follows the lovely River Stort.

ROUTE: Turn right out of Sawbridgeworth station, past **The Maltings** (**1**) and over two road bridges. Turn left along the side of the River Stort and stay on the towpath, crossing over a road.

Take the second waymarked footpath on the right, following a wooden walkway through marshland and a tree tunnel to a metal gate. Walk straight on across a field, through another gate into trees and bushes and finally turn left along a large avenue of oaks and chestnuts, above the rolling landscape of **Pishiobury Park** (**2**).

At the end of the avenue, carry on in the same direction onto a fenced path, with **Pishiobury House** (**3**) to your left. Cross Pishiobury Drive and go on beside a tall fence, turning right immediately after a stream and crossing two fields, bearing left to rejoin the river near **Harlow Mill** (**4**), once used for corn and flour, now a pub.

Continue to follow the towpath by the navigable River Stort, switching banks as convenient, all the way to Roydon. Just beyond **Harlow** (**5**), the workshops of **Parndon Mill** (**6**) have an interesting gallery on the ground floor. There are some riverside artworks nearby, including a walkway across the weir, decorated with glass and a sandstone sculpture called Flowing Onwards.

Although the path runs near the main road for a mile, it also has good views of Eastwick church across the river, and later of **Hunsdon Mead** (**7**) and other often-flooded fields, rich in wildlife. You reach **Roydon** (**8**), with a choice of cafés and a fine stone bridge, just after the seventh lock since Sawbridgeworth.

LOOK OUT FOR: The undulating landscape of **Pishiobury Park** (**2**), full of ancient avenues, wild flowers and long-horned cows, was partly designed by 'Capability' Brown, shortly before he died. It surrounds the 18th-century **Pishiobury House** (**3**). Henry VIII and then Anne Boleyn owned the earlier manor house here; the 'Oak Walk' is thought to date back to the 15th century.

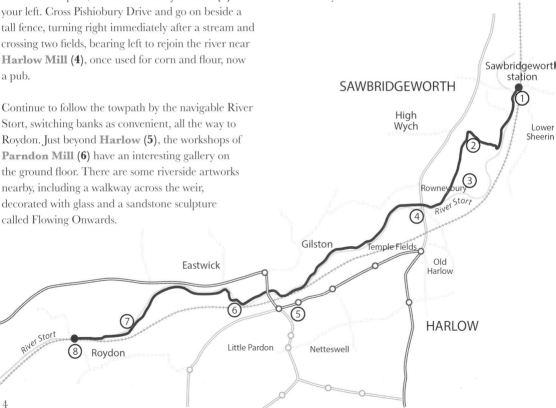

Above left: Pishiobury Park overflows with buttercups in May.
Above centre: The avenue known as 'Oak Walk' dates back to the 15th century.
Above right: Hunsdon Mead is rich in wildlife.

Modern Harlow (5) began as a pioneering new town in 1947. Before that, it was a small town with a collection of villages. Home to some of Britain's first post-war tower blocks and to dozens of public sculptures, including works by Henry Moore and Barbara Hepworth, it is full of surprising cultural treasures.

The delightful **Parndon Mill (6)** is a creative centre with numerous studios for artists and craftspeople. Painters, jewellers, carpenters, sculptors, printmakers and others work here every day. Local potter Sally Anderson rescued the derelict mill in 1968 and her creative vision has been thriving ever since, with changing exhibitions in the one-room gallery (http://www.parndonmill.co.uk/).

Hunsdon Mead (7) and other flowering fields lie on either side of the River Stort. The wildlife trust that manages this nature reserve describes it as 'one of the finest surviving areas of unimproved grassland in Eastern England'. Orchids, cowslips, kingcups and saxifrage are among the numerous wild flowers. Butterflies, herons, geese and overwintering fieldfares flock here, and you might even see traces of the local otters.

Roydon (8) is a riverside village with some old houses. The New Inn is an early 17th-century building and the nave of St Peter's church dates back to the 13th century.

FOOD AND DRINK: The Maltings, the sprawling, converted 19th-century complex opposite Sawbridgeworth station, is full of quirky shops and cafés and is worth exploring.

The pub at **Harlow Mill** makes a good stopping place right on the route (http://www.beefeatergrill.co.uk/beefeater/restaurants/chelmsford/harlow-mill.html). The Moorhen, across the river from Harlow Town station, has mixed reviews, but a pleasant location. There are several pubs at the end in Roydon, an authentic Italian restaurant in the old station waiting room and a bar in the Marina. You can even enjoy tea and cake outside **Roydon lock house**. Just ring the bell! (https://www.facebook.com/pages/Roydon-lock-house/211762228956703)

TRANSPORT: This section is well connected, passing four stations on the main line from London (Liverpool Street) to Cambridge, making it easy to divide into shorter walks. Harlow Town also has fast, regular Stansted Airport services. Cambridge trains stop every half an hour or so (less often on Sundays) at Sawbridgeworth and at Roydon station, which is right by the river.

Right: Sunset on the River Stort.

Roydon to Standon

12 miles

This relatively long, rural hike includes some beautiful views and ends in the pretty village of Standon.

From **Roydon** (**1**) level crossing, pass the station building on your left and take the footpath leading right along the edge of a field beside an avenue of chestnuts. At the far end of the field, the path heads right through a gate and then follows a wooden fence past a large, white house.

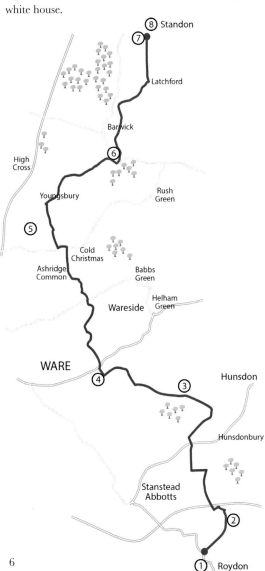

Cross the lawn next to a **little lake** (**2**) and follow the fence beyond until you reach a tarmac track. Turn briefly left along this and right onto a footpath signposted Hunsdon Road. The grassy path leads straight on and left round the edge of a field to find a tunnel under the main road.

Go through the tunnel and straight ahead under a row of pylons, admiring the views over distant Harlow to your right. Before you get to Olives Farm, which you can see in the valley below, turn left towards a little wood, skirt right round the end of the wood and cross the field towards Halfway House.

Cross the road, turn right through the farm buildings and left along a track towards trees. Turn right at the end of the wood and walk across fields, heading left when you reach a small pond and climbing towards **Moat Wood** (**3**).

Keep the wood on your right (the moat is in the bulge at the end) and carry on along a line of trees, turning right round the end of another wood and descending towards the Ash Valley. Passing another small but beautiful grove on your right, fork left towards picturesque Watersplace Farm.

Turn left along the track at the bottom (a disused railway) across the **River Ash** (**4**) and then right through the buildings up a stony track to a road. From here, this section of the Harcamlow follows the same route as the **Greenwich Meridian Trail** (GMT waymarks), which makes it easier to find your way.

Cross the road and go up the track ahead, past a farm, turning right in front of a white, weatherboard house. Walk down a green lane, cross a stream, turn left along the far side and right up the next field boundary towards a small wood. Carry on, with trees on your right, following a ditch on your left. In the next field, turn left quite soon to cross over another ditch and through another hedge, and follow the path diagonally right to a road.

Above left: Strolling down a country lane near Roydon.
Above centre: Beech wood near Barwick in the autumn.
Above right: The tower of Thundridge Old church, a magnet for ghost stories.

Cross the road and go along a track, soon passing between fences and finally bearing slightly right and downhill with views across the Rib Valley. Head downhill past a brick house to a road near the village of Cold Christmas. Turn left along this sunken lane and right on a hidden path signed to High Cross.

In winter you can see the tower of the **Thundridge Old church (5)** to the left through the trees. To visit it and the village of Thundridge, turn left along the river and follow the Hertfordshire Way. Otherwise, cross the river and go on uphill, eventually reaching Home Farm. The path straight on leads across the main road to High Cross, but the Harcamlow turns right towards a clump of trees.

Follow the track (still with GMT waymarks) as it winds past woods and heads downhill, turning left at the bottom towards the buildings and then right across **Barwick Ford (6)**. Cross the river and go up the road a little way until a sign points left to Latchford. Simply follow this track roughly northwards through woods and fields, bearing right on a tarmac lane and winding right and left through Latchford hamlet and finally straight on along a smaller lane towards the ford.

Carry on, bearing right, without crossing the ford and head uphill towards Standon, keeping right of the semicircular metal shed. There are good views of the River Rib and of a lovely Tudor mansion called **The Lordship (7)**. When the path eventually emerges onto Paper Mill Lane in **Standon (8)**, turn right towards the village.

LOOK OUT FOR: **Moat Wood (3)** is one of roughly 6,000 moated sites in England and would once have surrounded a manor house. Most of them were medieval status symbols rather than practical defences.

The **River Ash (4)** flows 16 miles from the village of Brent Pelham to Stanstead Abbots, where it joins the River Lee. The 19-mile **River Rib**, crossed twice in this day's walking, is another tributary of the Lee. The **Greenwich Meridian Trail** is a 270-mile walk that follows the line of the Prime Meridian, from the South Coast to East Yorkshire.

The tower of **Thundridge Old church (5)**, a small detour from the path, is another moated site, with all kinds of spooky tales attached to it.

The hamlet of Barwick, on the River Rib, north of **Barwick Ford (6)**, was built for the Smokeless Powders Company, which manufactured explosives in the late 19th century.

Elizabeth I once stayed in **The Lordship (7)**, which is the venue for the Standon Calling Festival each August (http://www.standon-calling.com/).

Standon (8) is a beautiful Hertfordshire village with huge numbers of listed buildings.

Above: A little lake near Roydon.

Above: Standon in the evening light.

FOOD AND DRINK: There's not much along this stretch, unless you venture off the track into Thundridge (which has several pubs and a lovely village café) or High Cross, with the welcoming White Horse (http://www.thewhitehorse-highcross.co.uk/), but Standon makes up for it with two great, down-to-earth pubs and a bakery-café, open until 4pm. Puckeridge, just north of Standon, across the main road, has further choices, including the new 'Something Lovely' tearoom, with its delicate china and home-made cakes (https://www.facebook.com/Somethinglovelytearoom).

TRANSPORT: Roydon has regular trains to London and Cambridge. Bus 700 connects Standon with Bishops Stortford and Bus 331 to Ware also goes through High Cross and Thundridge every couple of hours in case you want to break this section up. The Standon buses run mostly from the bus stops near the Heron Chinese restaurant, across the main road from the end of the walk.

Standon to Manuden

10 miles

This is another gently hilly walk with some good views, lovely woods and meadows, ending in a picturesque village.

From the Standon **pudding stone (1)** near the church, go east, past the old half-timbered, brick building, the village hall and almshouses. Where the lane swings right, carry on and turn left up a little tree tunnel path, which eventually drops down again past houses to the main road.

Cross carefully and turn right for 50m, then left onto a public bridleway, which leads up and downhill and eventually past the edge of a wood to a farm, with fine views. Follow the bridleway through the farmyard, right of the barn.

Turn left on the lane beyond the farm and immediately right through a gate. Walk parallel to the metal fence of beautiful **Upp Hall (2)**, with its 17th-century gables,

and then down the slope near a wooden fence and through a five-barred gate at the bottom.

When you reach a winding lane near the Tin House, turn left and follow it as far as a single Narnian lamppost and a signposted track to Cock Hampstead (among other places). Follow this – equally winding – track as it passes a radio mast and a house. When it veers left again, turn right across a field and then slightly left along a hedge towards a row of trees and beyond.

Eventually, near the houses of **Albury Hall (3)**, turn right towards a wood, and then follow the second waymark left off the lane along a beautiful if muddy path. Ironically, the local woods all seem to be named

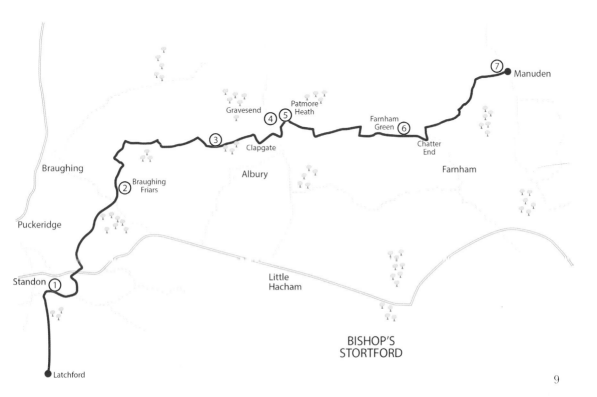

Above left: Patmore Heath is beautiful in any season.
Above centre: The path from Standon, through woods and fields.
Above right: Book exchange in Farnham Green phone box.

after British disasters. During the First World War the wood on the right was named after the Battle of Ypres; the wood nearer the hall is called Suez, presumably named sometime after 1956.

At a four-way footpath junction, go almost straight on, with the next, narrow wood on your left. The path veers right downhill and then left across the River Ash and back up to the road at Gravesend. The **Catherine Wheel pub** (**4**) is to the left, but the main route turns right off the road, by a letterbox, taking a fenced path to the corner of **Patmore Heath** (**5**).

Walk past or through the heath, turning right at a Hertfordshire Way sign between two houses. Follow the track downhill to the delightful Bog Cottage, then turn right on the track and almost immediately left on a path uphill signed to Albury (FP007).

Leave the Hertfordshire Way at the next junction, turning left towards trees. Cross a narrow footbridge and go straight on, skirting right and then left around Shaw Wood. As you reach the pylons beyond, you are crossing from Hertfordshire into Essex.

The track between fields becomes a lane at Shawwood Cottage. Follow this lane through **Farnham Green** (**6**), with its quirky book exchange in a phone box, and go on to the hamlet of Chatter End. Turn left at a footpath sign, next to a triangle with a faded cat sign, towards some sturdy oaks, cross another footbridge and turn right past a little grove.

Follow a muddy track, with a hedge on your right, as it eventually heads down to a stream, then uphill, with the hedge on the left. At the top of the hill, near Parsonage Farm, follow a waymark diagonally left across a field

Left: Dramatic skies above Manuden.

10

Above left: The church of St Mary the Virgin in Manuden.
Above centre: Beech trees in Manuden.
Above right: The Catherine Wheel is a good stopping place.

and eventually, following the hedge, out onto a lane. Go straight across the road onto a delightful wooded path and then right at the footpath junction (although the waymark only points left). Cross over when you reach a lane, heading downhill towards **Manuden (7)**. The path crosses a track, passes a graveyard and emerges near Manuden church.

LOOK OUT FOR: The Standon **pudding stone (1)** is an example of the pebbly, glacial rock geologically known as 'conglomerate'. It may have marked a prehistoric meeting place.

Patmore Heath (5) is a small, but lovely, area of grassy heathland, designated as a Site of Special Scientific Interest, due to its unusual combination of marshy and sandy habitats. Unusual grasses with great names like 'wavy hair', 'sheep's fescue' and 'sweet vernal' flourish here, along with bracken and bedstraw, rushes and spearwort. In the scattered ponds you might even spot newts, including the locally rare palmate newt.

Picturesque **Manuden village (7)** was famous for its yew trees, favoured by medieval arrow-makers. The flint-coated church dates back to the 12th century, but was rebuilt in Victorian times. Many of the houses are also medieval and still feature thatched roofs and overhanging lofts.

FOOD AND DRINK: **The Yew Tree pub** at Manuden has recently reopened to local acclaim and makes a perfect end to this walk. Standon and Stansted have pubs and cafes, and **The Catherine Wheel**, just off the route at Gravesend, makes a great lunch stop, opening daily at midday (http://www.thecatherinewheelalbury.co.uk/).

TRANSPORT: For **Standon** buses see the previous chapter. There is currently just one rather erratic bus per day to and from **Albury** and Gravesend (the number 20, which shuttles between Bishops Stortford and 'the Pelhams' around noon). If you're really organised, you could use this to divide the section in half.

Manuden is a couple of miles from **Stansted Mountfichet**, which has a main-line train station and several buses. Alternatively, a taxi from Manuden to Stansted Town or Bishops Stortford costs about £10 and could be quite economical if shared (Stortford's Associated Taxis are very reliable, 01279 655666).

Above: A pub lunch on the way.

Manuden to Newport

8 miles

Thatched cottages, ancient chapels and bluebell woods are highlights of this pleasant walk.

From **Manuden church** (**1**), take the little lane near the pub across a bridge and turn left along the River Stort. Very soon, turn right along a path that looks like a private drive, skirt round a bungalow and head uphill on a grassy path. At the top, go on across a field and turn left along the next hedge, and follow this path round to the right again until eventually you reach a track near **Bollington Hall** (**2**).

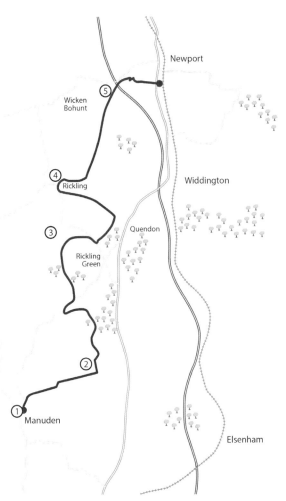

Turn left along this track, keeping left of 16th-century Wade's Hall and following the left-hand side of Broom Wood. Fork left through trees, around the end of a smaller wood, and then follow a winding path, heading west to emerge eventually onto a minor road. Turn right on the road and, when the power lines cross overhead, turn left onto a footpath. (Alternatively, you can follow the lane into delightful **Rickling Green**.)

The path runs along the left-hand end of Catherine Grove, turns briefly left and then right near another wood, following the hedge, then a ditch and a lane towards **Rickling Hall** (**3**) in the valley. Turn right after the first barn along a grassy track with a hedge on the left towards more buildings.

Turn right along the lane at the end and then left onto a bridleway along the side of a wood, just before the next house. This wood has carpets of snowdrops in February and bluebells in May. Follow the track beside a field, with the white bell tower of Quendon church just visible through the trees to the right, and then turn left uphill through an avenue. Cross a track at the end of the avenue and go straight on along a field path, through a gap in the hedge and on, beside a ditch, to a road.

Turn right towards **All Saints church** (**4**) and right again in front of it, passing two beautiful thatched cottages and a modern barn on your left. Go on in this direction along a winding, gravel track. When the track swings left, ignore the right turn and go on down a rutted, tree-lined lane.

Finally, a yellow waymark points left into a field. Follow the path down to a bridge and some buildings, including the ancient **St Helen's Chapel** (**5**).

Above left: Bluebells in Quendon Woods.
Above centre: The white bell tower of Quendon church is just visible.
Above right: St Helen's Chapel, one of the oldest buildings in eastern England.

Continue, right and then left through the houses, to reach a road and turn right under the M11. Cross a stream and, immediately afterwards, turn diagonally right across a field to a gap in the hedge. Cross a ditch and go on past a small grove, eventually emerging between houses onto a road. Turn right, then left and simply carry on in this direction, crossing over Newport High Street, to reach the station.

LOOK OUT FOR: **Rickling Hall (3)** was originally a moated castle and the oldest parts of the building date from the 14th century. This lovely red-brick farmhouse is just one of many listed buildings in the area: others include thatched Apple Tree Cottage in Rickling and Monk's Barn on Newport High Street.

The villages of **Rickling** and **Rickling Green** were so called after a 6th-century queen of Essex called Ricola; the name Richelinga meant 'Ricola's people'. The welcoming Cricketers Arms (just off the route) looks out across the village green.

All Saints church (4) at Rickling is a 13th-century flint church, but its unusual layout suggests pre-Norman origins. There are several ancient features, like the 15th-century wooden pulpit and the Victorian stained glass.

St Helen's Chapel (5) dates from the 11th (or possibly even 10th) century and is one of the oldest surviving buildings in eastern England. A Bronze Age settlement was excavated near this Norman chapel of thatch, pebble and flint with its tiny windows.

FOOD AND DRINK: **The Cricketers Arms** (http://www.thecricketersarmsricklinggreen.co.uk/) at Rickling Green makes a great stopping point.

Newport's High Street, at the end, has further options: Saggers' garden centre does brilliantly cheap self-service tea and cakes (Suzie's Teas) upstairs with a view of the plants and statues. Of **Newport**'s two pubs, the White Horse is closer to the station. Nearer still is the Radhuni Indian restaurant and historic Dorringtons Bakery, with a café area.

TRANSPORT: See p.11 for transport to Manuden. **Newport** has local buses and regular trains to London, Cambridge and stations in between. The 301 bus runs hourly from Saffron Walden to Bishops Stortford via Quendon, making it an excellent place to divide the walk.

Above: Walking up from Manuden.

Above: Apple Tree Cottage in Rickling.

Newport to Thaxted

8 miles

This ramble passes through pretty Debden and ends in the colourful town of Thaxted.

Cross the railway away from **Newport** (**1**) and turn left along the lane behind the station. Take the first path on the right, follow it uphill towards a fence and continue along this path with hedges or fences on your left as it zigzags upwards, coming out onto a road. Cross the road, turn briefly left and then right down a hedged path, which runs through a wood and across a field.

Turn right just before a stream, **Debden Water** (**2**), and follow this path through pleasant, undulating fields until you reach a road. Turn right along this busy road and left through Debden Park, heading downhill towards the lake.

Turn left by the lake and immediately right along the path into the churchyard of **St Mary the Virgin** (**3**) in Debden. The lane on the far side leads up into the village, passing the Yuva restaurant in the former White Hart pub.

Just beyond Yuva, take the left-hand lane, which becomes a track, passing Deynes House (with a psychedelic cow in the garden) and continues across open fields, eventually reaching **Rowney Wood** (**4**). Follow the edge of the wood, keeping it on your left, and walk roughly straight on, then left and then right, finally leaving the wood behind and heading over fields and along a muddy track until you reach Page's Farm.

Turn left beyond the farm and follow the field boundary until it veers left and you carry on across a field, over a stream and under a row of pylons. Beyond the stream, follow a hedge uphill until an arrow points right into a **machinery yard** (**5**). Walk through the avenue of ploughs and tractors, turn left, then briefly right through a gate and left again along a concrete lane. Turn right through a small wood opposite the farmhouse and cross a stream.

Keep straight on across a field and then left along the next hedge, right a little way, then left again along a tree tunnel and straight on, with a hedge on the left. When you reach a house, turn right along a concrete track beside the infant River Chelmer, which eventually becomes the lane uphill into **Thaxted** (**6**).

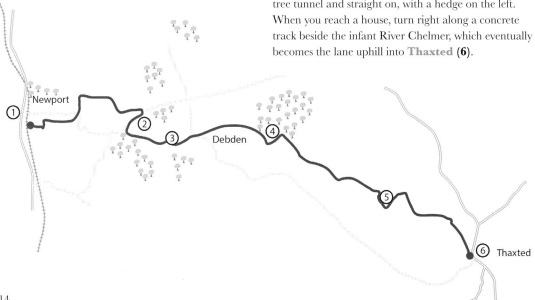

Above left: Debden Village.
Above centre: The blossom-bordered path from Newport.
Above right: Yuva restaurant in the former White Hart pub.

LOOK OUT FOR: **St Mary's church** (**3**) in Debden dates from the 13th century; the pillars in the nave are the oldest part of the building and the porch you walk in through was added around 1340, but lots of things were added later, like the Victorian stained glass. The pretty wooden steeple was replaced in 1930; in spring, the churchyard is carpeted with snowdrops.

Debden Village is full of delightful cottages; its original name was Depeduna, meaning 'deep valley'.

Rowney Wood (**4**) is quite old, but the Forestry Commission has replanted some of it with conifers. It still has a lot of wildlife and you can see bluebells and even oxlips in season.

The **River Chelmer** starts very close to the route here and flows through Essex to join the River Blackwater near Maldon and then into the North Sea.

The wonderful town of **Thaxted** (**6**) is one of the highlights of the route. It has a cathedral-like church at the top of hilly Town Street, a half-timbered, medieval guildhall, cobbled lanes, colourful almshouses and more. It's worth scheduling an hour or so just to have a look around.

FOOD AND DRINK: **Yuva** in Debden is recommended; its Indo-Nepalese fusion cuisine is a cut above usual curry-house fare, with fresh Himalayan specialities and a weekday lunch deal (http://w-byte.com/ yuvadebden/index.html). Debden also boasts a community shop and the Plough pub.

Thaxted is well supplied with pubs and cafés. **Parrishes** on Town Street does sandwiches, cream teas and even a full Sunday roast (http://www. parrishes.co.uk/). **Poppy's** tearoom is open at the weekends, serving prize-winning cakes like double ginger, rhubarb and cinnamon or orange chocolate drizzle (http://www.poppystearoom.co.uk/).

TRANSPORT: **Newport** is on the London–Cambridge railway line. Debden and Thaxted are served by the eccentric, but reliable, number 6 bus, which winds between Saffron Walden and Bishops Stortford, calling at an extraordinary number of villages.

Below left: Debden churchyard in February.
Below centre: Colourful houses on Watling Street.
Below right: Another cheerful cottage in Thaxted.

Thaxted to Takeley

10 miles

**Walk through rolling countryside, along the River Chelmer
and past the site of Tilty's Cistercian abbey.**

From the Swan in Thaxted, walk right past the imposing **church** (**1**) through the two colourful almshouses behind it, and follow the church-yard wall towards the **windmill** (**2**). Continue straight on, passing the windmill on your right and heading gently downhill to a road. Turn briefly left, along the road past a house, and then right over a little hidden footbridge.

Turn right again in the field, follow a ditch to the corner, and then turn left along the little **River Chelmer** (**3**). Follow the river all the way to Duton Hill, crossing over Folly Mill Lane after nearly a mile and going on past lines of willows and tufted reed beds.

Emerging through a garden onto the road at **Duton Hill** (**4**), the delightful Three Horseshoes pub is nearby, uphill to the left. Otherwise, turn right to the bridge, cross over at the T-junction and take the path beyond, straight on beside a stream.

Turn left just before a wood and go across a field up a path, which becomes a track by a derelict mill. Turn left by the mill through a gate and then right up a field past the diminutive ruins of **Tilty Abbey** to the **church** (**5**) beyond. It is definitely worth popping into the church, which is usually open (take off muddy boots).

Go along the lane past the church, and the unusual, curved Abbey Gates House, and turn right along the road. Just before a house on the left, take a footpath leading left down through fields to a road, skirting right and then left round the last field.

Cross the road and find a little bridge in the bottom right-hand corner of the paddock beyond. Cross this and climb again to another road. Turn right along this quiet lane until it swings

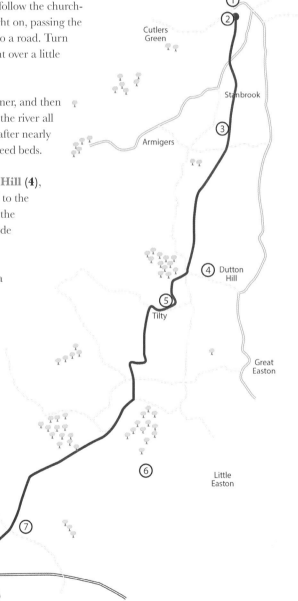

Above left: Almshouses by Thaxted church.
Above centre: The beautiful old east window in Tilty church.
Above right: The ruins of Tilty Abbey at sunset.

right and you turn left along a muddy track, soon forking right along a tree tunnel. Two left turns here instead would bring you out near **Easton Lodge (6)**.

Follow the main path through a wood, across a field, and bear slightly left to reach **Bamber's Green (7)**. Carry on across the crossroads, over the A120 along the same road, until you reach the B1256 and turn left to the Four Ashes pub and bus stops.

LOOK OUT FOR: If you didn't have time to explore **Thaxted** at the end of the last stage, do have a stroll around before you set off. Gustav Holst lived here from 1913, composed part of 'The Planets' and founded the local music festival. There is a plaque on the wall of his music room in Town Street, near a seasonal information centre (http://www.thaxted.co.uk/content/tourism).

Thaxted's grand, airy, **medieval church (1)**, with its ancient stained glass, has been described as the finest parish church in England and the 'Cathedral of Essex' (http://www.thaxtedparishchurch.co.uk/).

John Webb's windmill (2), built in 1804, is open at weekends from Easter to September (http://www.thaxted.co.uk/content/windmill).

The **Church of St Mary the Virgin (5)** at **Tilty** was once the gatehouse chapel of a huge **Cistercian abbey**, whose ruins you can see in the field below. The abbey was destroyed in 1536, but signboards at either end of the field tell you about its history. The church itself also has several interesting features, including a beautiful east window with elaborate stone tracery (one of the best in England, apparently) and an old, beamed ceiling.

Above: The windmill and Church of St John the Baptist in Thaxted.

Right: Much of the route is along old tracks with flowering hedgerows.

Above left: A pretty cottage garden in Takeley.
Above centre: Another picturesque cottage in Takeley.
Above right: The Four Ashes pub in Takeley stands opposite a Bronze Age sarsen stone on the village green.

The heritage-listed gardens at **Easton Lodge** (**6**) have been restored by volunteers and are open to the public a few times a year. In the 19th century, they belonged to a socialist countess called Daisy and early 20th-century visitors included Gustav Holst (who lived in Thaxted), George Bernard Shaw and the novelist H.G. Wells, who lived on the estate.

Bamber's Green (**7**) is a delightful hamlet with some thatched cottages and farms. Bury Farmhouse, by the crossroads, has 16th-century timber framing with a half-hipped roof and brick chimneystack.

There are further lovely houses on the road into **Takeley** (**8**), which has a very active local history society, who have published several booklets.

FOOD AND DRINK: Just left of the path at Duton Hill, the **Three Horseshoes** is worth the detour for a

drink (real ale; no food). Friendly and full of collections of retro signs and old bottles, it's a brilliantly quirky place to take a break. Even the ladies' loo is crammed with feminist quotes. You might want to check opening hours if you're relying on it, by calling 01371 870681. Otherwise, you'll need to keep going to the Four Ashes at Takeley (http://thefourashes.co.uk/), which does no-nonsense food at reasonable prices.

TRANSPORT: The number 5/6 bus from Bishops Stortford, via Stansted Airport, mentioned in the previous chapter, gets to Thaxted in the end (but not on Sundays). From Takeley, there are several other buses, including the 301 and 308 to Stortford and the 133 between Stansted and Braintree (Sundays too). The (infrequent) 312, from Saffron Walden to Great Dunmow, passes through Duton Hill if you want to split this section in half.

Left: The Three Horseshoes in Duton Hill.

Takeley to Sawbridgeworth

8 miles

Walk through Hatfield Forest and a series of historic villages en route to the River Stort.

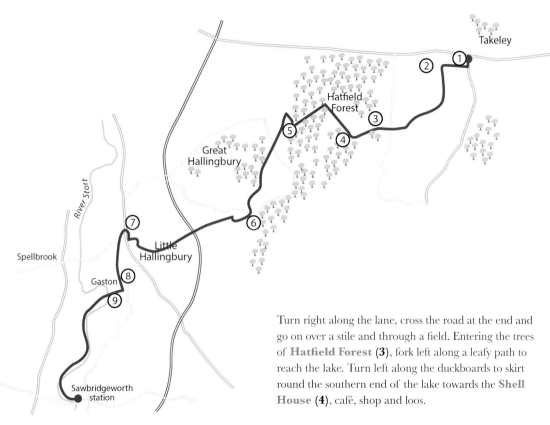

From the Four Ashes pub in Takeley, cross the main road, passing the Bronze Age **sarsen stone** (**1**) on the green, and turn left around the old station house, doubling back to the right along the **Flitch Way** (**2**)

At the end of the tree-hidden houses, turn left along a waymarked path and follow it as it curves right past a pond. When the path reaches trees, turn left through the hedge and diagonally right across a field towards the hamlet of Bush End.

Turn right along the lane, cross the road at the end and go on over a stile and through a field. Entering the trees of **Hatfield Forest** (**3**), fork left along a leafy path to reach the lake. Turn left along the duckboards to skirt round the southern end of the lake towards the **Shell House** (**4**), café, shop and loos.

On the far side of the buildings, a tarmac track runs parallel to the lake. Follow this until, soon after a gravel drive signed to Warren House, a series of yellow-topped marker posts leads left away from the road across open country. Following these posts roughly north-westwards towards more trees brings you, through some bushes, to one end of a broad woodland ride.

Turn left along this to the end and then right along the edge of the forest. Turn left through a wooden gate by some buildings and on between beech hedges. Turn left again through another gate, past a small orchard and along the edge of another **lake** (**5**), Beggars Hall fishing club.

Above left: Hatfield Forest has open spaces as well as trees.
Above centre: The lake has boats for hire in summer.
Above right: Canal boats along the navigable River Stort.

At the end of the lake, take the path in the far right corner straight on over a footbridge and through some houses to emerge onto a lane next to picturesque Street Farm Cottage, with its thatched roof and diamond-leaded windows.

Cross the road slightly leftwards and take the path, across a stile, going straight on along the right-hand edge of a field. Cross a stile and footbridge and take the path ahead through a cornfield to some trees. Turn left beside the trees and – when they end – go diagonally right across fields to the corner of a wooden fence.

Keep this fence on your left and follow it to a hedge. The lovely meadow-circled village beyond is **Woodside Green** (**6**). Head diagonally right across the grass towards the big chestnut tree by the nearest houses. Turn right along the lane, passing houses on your left, until just after Cobbs Barn a signposted path leads left.

Go through three gates, across a field, and over the M11. Keep on along the right-hand edge of a field, skirt left and then right around a grass-banked reservoir. Continue left-right-left onto a path beside a ditch leading towards **Little Hallingbury** (**7**) on the hill ahead.

Near the houses, turn right, then left across a footbridge and right again along the main road at the top to the George Inn. Turn left along Dell Lane (signposted Spellbrook) and, when the road swings right, carry on along a path ahead through two fields and round the left-hand edge of a third, eventually passing **Gaston House** (**8**) on the left and emerging, via a gravel track, onto a country lane.

Turn right down the lane to **Hallingbury Mill** (**9**) and take the path beyond it across meadows and over a footbridge to the lock. From here, simply turn left

Left: A pretty cottage in Little Hallingbury.